PIANO · VOCAL · GUITAR

W9-DEB-845

COUNTRY INSPIRATION

This publication is not for sale in
the EC and/or Australia
or New Zealand.

ISBN 0-7935-2156-4

HAL·LEONARD™
CORPORATION
7777 W. BLUEMOUND RD. P.O. BOX 13819 MILWAUKEE, WI 53213

Copyright © 1993 by HAL LEONARD CORPORATION
International Copyright Secured   All Rights Reserved

For all works contained herein:
Unauthorized copying, arranging, adapting, recording or public performance is an infringement of copyright.
Infringers are liable under the law.

BROTHERLY LOVE

Words and Music by JIMMY STEWART
and TIM NICHOLS

Copyright © 1989 Milsap Music, Inc., Talbot Music and Peer-International Company
Rights for Milsap Music, Inc. administered by Careers-BMG Music Publishing, Inc. (BMI)
International Copyright Secured   All Rights Reserved

- thin'   we____   all____   need._____

CODA

they've got some - thin' spe - cial, it's broth - er - ly love.__

Yeah,

rit.

DADDY'S HANDS

Words and Music by HOLLY DUNN

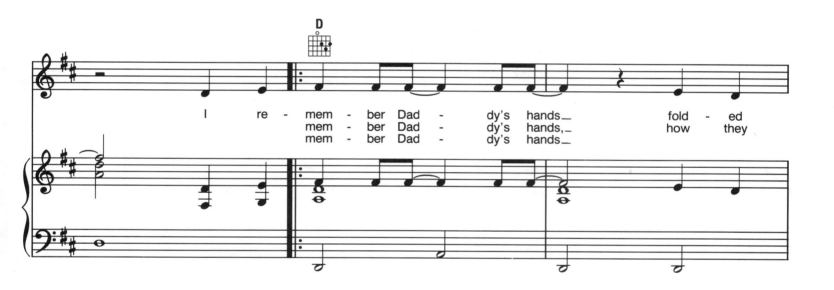

Copyright © 1986 EMI BLACKWOOD MUSIC INC.
All Rights Reserved   International Copyright Secured   Used by Permission

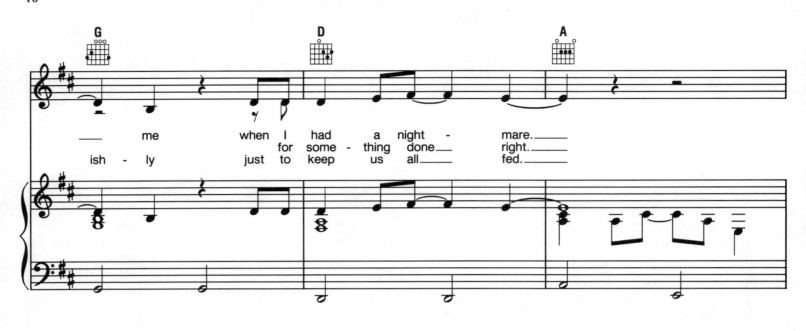

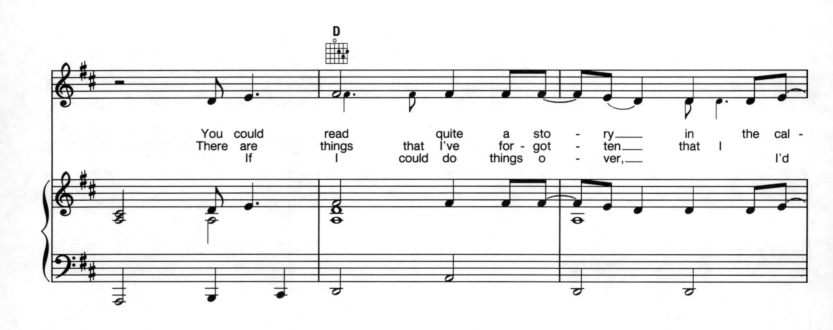

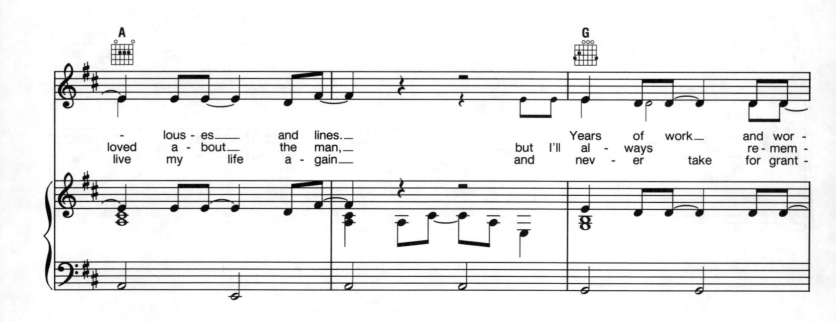

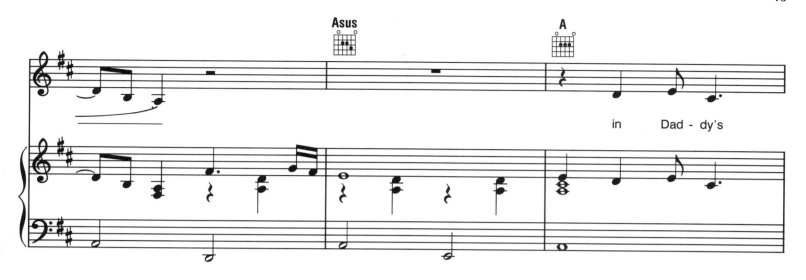

in   Dad - dy's

hands.

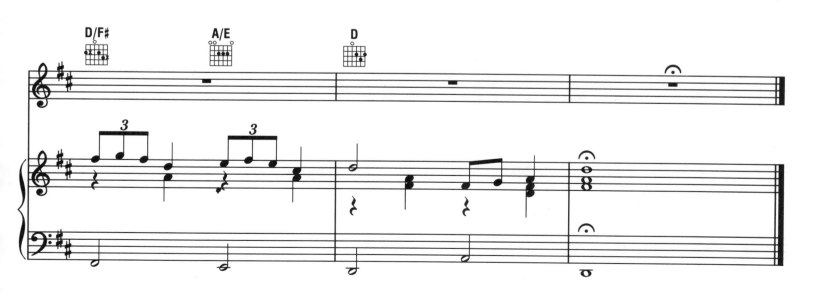

EVERYDAY

Words and Music by DAVE LOGGINS
and J.D. MARTIN

Moderately Fast (♪♪ is played ♪³♪)

You know a

smile nev - er goes out of style,__ so bright - en up the one that you wear.__
kind word nev - er goes un - heard,__ but too of - ten goes un - said.__

Let it shine__ and you just__ might find,__ you'll
And on the tongue__ of the old__ and the young,__ it's

© Copyright 1984 by LEEDS MUSIC CORPORATION, PATCHWORK MUSIC, and MUSIC CORPORATION OF AMERICA, INC.
Rights Administered by MCA MUSIC PUBLISHING, A Division of MCA INC., 1755 Broadway, New York, NY 10019
International Copyright Secured   All Rights Reserved
MCA music publishing

GOD BLESS THE U.S.A.

Words and Music by
LEE GREENWOOD

Slowly

Verse

(1.) If to-mor-row all the things were gone I'd worked for all my life, And I

had to start a-gain ___ with just my chil-dren and my wife. I'd

© Copyright 1984 by MUSIC CORPORATION OF AMERICA, INC. and SONGS OF POLYGRAM INTERNATIONAL, INC.
Rights administered by MCA MUSIC PUBLISHING, A Division of MCA INC., 1755 Broadway, New York, NY 10019
International Copyright Secured   All Rights Reserved
MCA music publishing

GUARDIAN ANGELS

Words and Music by NAOMI JUDD,
JOHN JARVIS and DON SCHLITZ

Copyright © 1989 Plugged In Music (BMI), Kentucky Sweetheart (BMI), Don Schlitz Music (ASCAP) and Almo Music
Plugged In Music (BMI) Administered by Bug Music Inc.
International Copyright Secured   All Rights Reserved

GRANDPA
(TELL ME 'BOUT THE GOOD OLD DAYS)

Medium Slow Country

Words and Music by JAMIE O'HARA

Grand-pa, tell me 'bout the good old days._
Grand-pa, ev-'ry-thing is chang-in' fast._

Some-times ____ it feels ____ like this world's gone cra-
We call ____ it prog-ress, but I just don't know._

Copyright © 1985 by Cross Keys Publishing Co., Inc.
All Rights Administered by Sony Music Publishing, 8 Music Square West, Nashville, TN 37203
International Copyright Secured   All Rights Reserved

Oh, ____ oh, ____ grand - pa, ____ tell ____ me 'bout the good old ____ days. ____

D.S. and Fade

Did fam - 'lies real - ly

I SAW THE LIGHT

Words and Music by
HANK WILLIAMS

Copyright © 1948 by Acuff-Rose-Opryland Music, Inc.
Copyright Renewed, Assigned to Acuff-Rose-Opryland Music, Inc. and Aberbach Enterprises, Ltd. (Rightsong Music, Administrator) for the U.S.A. only
All rights outside the U.S.A. controlled by Acuff-Rose-Opryland Music, Inc.
International Copyright Secured   All Rights Reserved

I WON'T TAKE LESS THAN YOUR LOVE

Moderately bright country

Words and Music by DON SCHLITZ
and PAUL OVERSTREET

"How much do I owe you," said the husband to his wife,
"How much do I owe you," said the man to his Lord,

"for standing beside me and through the
"forgiving me this day and ev'ry

hard years of my life?
day that's gone before?

Shall I bring you
Shall I build you a tem-

© Copyright 1987, 1988 by MCA MUSIC PUBLISHING, A Division of MCA INC., DON SCHLITZ MUSIC, WRITERS GROUP MUSIC and SCARLET MOON MUSIC
Rights of DON SCHLITZ MUSIC administered by MCA MUSIC PUBLISHING, A Division of MCA INC., 1755 Broadway, New York, NY 10019
International Copyright Secured   All Rights Reserved
MCA music publishing

All the rich - es of the world_____ could
All the trea - sures of the world_____ could

Dm   Bb   C
To Coda ⊕

nev - er be e - nough,_____ and I won't take less than your love."__
nev - er be e - nough,_____ and I

F   C

"How much do I owe,_____ you," to the

42

moth - er said the son, _____ "for all that you __ have taught me in the days when I was ___ young? ___ Shall I bring ex - pen - sive blan - kets to cast up - on ___ your bed, _____ And a pil - low for to rest ___ your ___ wear - y head?" ___ And the moth - er said, "I

I'M NO STRANGER TO THE RAIN

Words and Music by SONNY CURTIS
and RON HELLARD

Copyright © 1986 Tree Publishing Co., Inc.
All Rights Administered by Sony Music Publishing, 8 Music Square West, Nashville, TN 37203
International Copyright Secured   All Rights Reserved

52

SOMEBODY UP THERE LIKES ME

Words and Music by SUZY WILLS
and BILL COOLEY

Copyright © 1989 PolyGram International Publishing, Inc. and Reba McEntire Music
International Copyright Secured   All Rights Reserved

KEEP IT BETWEEN THE LINES

Words and Music by RUSSELL SMITH
and KATHY LOUVIN

Moderate four-beat

He was

sit - tin' be - side___ me in the pas - sen - ger seat as I
sit - tin' in my chair,___ kind - a sneak - in' a look at him
fin - ished the pic - ture and I put him to bed. Got

looked through the wind - shield at the qui - et lit - tle street. He was
ly - in' on the floor___ with his col - or - ing book. Then he
down on my knees___ and I bowed my head. And I said,

© Copyright 1991 by MCA MUSIC PUBLISHING, A Division of MCA INC., 1755 Broadway, New York, NY 10019 and TILLIS TUNES, INC.
International Copyright Secured All Rights Reserved
MCA music publishing

59

Be - lieve in the things___ that are real.___

Take___ your___ time and keep it be - tween_____ the lines.___

Just take___ your___ time ___ and

keep it be - tween_____ the lines.___

rit.

THE LAST GAME OF THE SEASON
(THE BLIND MAN IN THE BLEACHERS)

Words and Music by
STERLING WHIPPLE

(Spoken:) He's just the blind man in the bleachers to the local home town fans, And he sits beneath the speakers way back in the stands, And he listens to the play by play; waitin' for one

Copyright © 1975 by Tree Publishing Co., Inc.
All Rights Administered by Sony Music Publishing, 8 Music Square West, Nashville, TN 37203
International Copyright Secured   All Rights Reserved

LORD, I HOPE THIS DAY IS GOOD

Words and Music by
DAVE HANNER

Lord,_____ I hope this day is good,____
Lord,_____ have you for - got - ten me?____

I'm feel - ing emp - ty and mis - un - der - stood;____
I've been pray - in' to you faith - ful - ly.____

Copyright © 1981 Sabal Music
All Rights Administered by PolyGram International Publishing, Inc.
International Copyright Secured   All Rights Reserved

LOVE CAN BUILD A BRIDGE

Words and Music by JOHN JARVIS,
PAUL OVERSTREET and NAOMI JUDD

Copyright © 1990 Inspector Barlow Music (ASCAP), Scarlet Moon Music and Kentucky Sweetheart Music (BMI)
All Rights for Inspector Barlow Music (ASCAP) Administered by Bug Music Inc.
International Copyright Secured   All Rights Reserved

78

LOVE WITHOUT END, AMEN

Words and Music by
AARON G. BARKER

Copyright © 1990 O-Tex Music (BMI) and Bill Butler Music (BMI)
1000 18th Avenue South, Nashville, TN 37212
International Copyright Secured All Rights Reserved

81

MIRACLES

Words and Music by
ROGER COOK

Moderately slow, in 2

mf

with ped. throughout

Mir-a-cles, mir-a-cles,___ that's what life's a-bout.

Most of___ you must a-gree___ if you've thought it out.___

I can see and I___ can hear,___ I can tell___ you why
Well who is rich and who___ is poor,___ who has more___ than me?

Copyright © 1976, 1982 Dick James Music Ltd.
All rights for the United States and Canada controlled by Songs Of PolyGram International, Inc.
International Copyright Secured   All Rights Reserved

A THING CALLED LOVE

Words and Music by
JERRY REED

Copyright © 1968 Sixteen Stars Music and Vector Music
International Copyright Secured   All Rights Reserved

YOU'RE MY BEST FRIEND

Words and Music by
WAYLAND HOLYFIELD

Copyright © 1975 PolyGram International Publishing, Inc.
International Copyright Secured   All Rights Reserved

THE VOWS GO UNBROKEN
(ALWAYS TRUE TO YOU)

Words and Music by GARY BURR
and ERIC KAZ

© Copyright 1988 by MCA MUSIC PUBLISHING, A Division of MCA INC., GARY BURR MUSIC, and ZENA MUSIC
Rights of GARY BURR MUSIC administered by MCA MUSIC PUBLISHING, A Division of MCA INC., 1755 Broadway, New York, NY 10019.
International Copyright Secured   All Rights Reserved

MCA music publishing

WHY ME?
A.K.A. WHY ME, LORD?

Words and Music by
KRIS KRISTOFFERSON

Moderately, with a Gospel feeling

© 1972 RESACA MUSIC PUBLISHING CO.
All Rights Controlled and Administered by EMI BLACKWOOD MUSIC INC.
All Rights Reserved   International Copyright Secured   Used by Permission

YOU DON'T COUNT THE COST

Words and Music by BUCKY JONES,
CHRIS WATERS and TOM SHAPIRO

Copyright © 1991 PolyGram International Publishing, Inc., McBEC Music, Edge O' Woods Music, Kinetic Diamond Music, Inc. and Moline Valley Music, Inc.
International Copyright Secured   All Rights Reserved

Your Favorites in COUNTRY MUSIC

#1 COUNTRY SONGS OF THE 80'S
44 Chart-topping country hits, including: American Made • Any Day Now • Could I Have This Dance • Crying My Heart Out Over You • Forever And Ever Amen • Forty Hour Week (For A Livin') • Grandpa (Tell Me 'Bout The Good Old Days) • He Stopped Loving Her Today • I Was In The Stream • My Heroes Have Always Been Cowboys • Smoky Mountain Rain • Why Not Me • You're The Reason God Made Oklahoma.
_____00360715 $12.95

80'S LADIES—TOP HITS FROM COUNTRY WOMEN OF THE 80'S
23 songs by today's female country stars including: Roseanne Cash, Crystal Gayle, The Judds, Reba McEntire, Anne Murray, K.T. Oslin and others. Songs include: I Don't Know Why You Don't Want Me • Lyin' In His Arms Again • Why Not Me • A Sunday Kind Of Love • Could I Have This Dance • Do'Ya • Strong Enough To Bend.
_____00359741 $9.95

THE AWARD-WINNING SONGS OF THE COUNTRY MUSIC ASSOCIATION First Edition
All of the official top five songs nominated for the CMA "Song Of The Year" from 1967 to 1983. 85 selections, featuring: Always On My Mind • Behind Closed Doors • Don't It Make My Brown Eyes Blue • Elvira • The Gambler • I.O.U. • Mammas Don't Let Your Babies Grow Up To Be Cowboys • Swingin' • You're The Reason God Made Oklahoma.
_____00359485 $16.95

AWARD-WINNING SONGS OF THE COUNTRY MUSIC ASSOCIATION Second Edition – Updated
An update to the first edition, this songbook features 35 songs nominated for "Song Of The Year" by the Country Music Association from 1984 through 1991. Songs include: Islands In The Stream • Chiseled In Stone • Don't Rock The Jukebox • Friends In Low Places • God Bless The U.S.A. • Grandpa (Tell Me 'Bout The Good Old Days) • All My Ex's Live In Texas • Forever And Ever, Amen.
_____00312476 $16.95

THE NEW ULTIMATE COUNTRY FAKE BOOK
More than 700 of the greatest country hits of all-time. Includes an alphabetical index and an artist index! Includes: Cold, Cold Heart • Crazy • Crying My Heart Out Over You • Daddy Sang Bass • Diggin' Up Bones • God Bless The U.S.A. • Grandpa (Tell Me 'Bout The Good Old Days) • Great Balls Of Fire • Green, Green Grass Of Home • He Stopped Loving Her Today • I.O.U. • I Was Country When Country Wasn't Cool • I Wouldn't Have Missed It For The World • Lucille • Mammas Don't Let Your Babies Grow Up To Be Cowboys • On The Other Hand • Ruby, Don't Take Your Love To Town • Swingin' • Talking In Your Sleep • Through The Years • Whoever's In New England • Why Not Me • You Needed Me • and MORE!
_____00240049 $35.00

THE BEST COUNTRY SONGS EVER
We've updated this outstanding collection of country songs to include even more of your favorites—over 75 in all! Featuring: Always On My Mind • Behind Closed Doors • Could I Have This Dance • Crazy • Daddy Sang Bass • D-I-V-O-R-C-E • Forever And Ever, Amen • God Bless The U.S.A. • Grandpa (Tell Me 'Bout The Good Old Days) • Help Me Make It Through The Night • I Fall To Pieces • If We Make It Through December • Jambalaya (On The Bayou) • Love Without End, Amen • Mammas Don't Let Your Babies Grow Up To Be Cowboys • Stand By Your Man • Through The Years • and more. Features stay-open binding.
_____00359135 $16.95

THE GREAT AMERICAN COUNTRY SONGBOOK
The absolute best collection of top country songs anywhere. 70 titles, featuring: Any Day Now • Could I Have This Dance • Heartbroke • I Was Country When Country Wasn't Cool • I'm Gonna Hire A Wino To Decorate Our Home • It's Hard To Be Humble • Jambalaya • Smokey Mountain Rain • Through The Years • many others.
_____00359947 $12.95

COUNTRY LOVE SONGS
25 Sentimental country favorites, including: Could I Have This Dance • Forever And Ever, Amen • She Believes In Me • Through The Years • The Vows Go Unbroken • You Decorated My Life • You Needed Me • and more.
_____00311528 $9.95

For more information, see your local music dealer, or write to:
Hal Leonard Publishing Corporation
P.O. Box 13819 Milwaukee, Wisconsin 53213

51 COUNTRY STANDARDS
A collection of 51 of country's biggest hits including: (Hey Won't You Play) Another Somebody Done Somebody Wrong Song • By The Time I Get To Phoenix • Could I Have This Dance • Daddy Sang Bass • Forever And Ever, Amen • Bless The U.S.A. • Green, Green Grass Of Home • Islands In The Stream • King Of The Road • Little Green Apples • Lucille • Mammas Don't Let Your Babies Grow Up To Be Cowboys • Ruby Don't Take Your Love To Town • Stand By Me • Through The Years • Your Cheatin' Heart.
_____00359517 $10.95

COUNTRY MUSIC HALL OF FAME
The Country Music Hall Of Fame Was Founded in 1961 by the Country Music Association (CMA). Each Year, new members are elected—and these books are the first to represent all of its members with photos, biography and music selections related to each individual.

Volume 1
Includes: Fred Rose, Hank Williams, Jimmie Rodgers, Roy Acuff, George D. Hay, PeeWee King, Minnie Pearl and Grandpa Jones. 23 songs, including: Blue Eyes Crying In The Rain • Cold, Cold Heart • Wabash Cannon Ball • Tennesse Waltz.
_____00359510 $8.95

Volume 2
Features: Tex Ritter, Ernest Tubb, Eddy Arnold, Jim Denny, Joseph Lee Frank, Uncle Dave Macon, Jim Reeves and Bill Monroe. Songs include: Jealous Heart • Walking The Floor Over You • Make The World Go Away • Ruby, Don't Take Your Love To Town • Kentucky Waltz • Is It Really Over • many more.
_____00359504 $8.95

Volume 3
Red Foley, Steve Sholes, Bob Wills, Gene Autry, Original Carter Family, Arthur Satherley, Jimmie Davis and The Orginal Sons Of The Pioneers. 24 songs: Peace In The Valley • Ashes Of Love • San Antonio Rose • Tumbling Tumble Weeds • Born To Lose • Worried Man's Blues • many more.
_____00359508 $8.95

Volume 4
Features: Chet Atkins, Patsy Cline, Owen Bradley, Kitty Wells, Hank Snow, Hubert Long, Connie B. Gay and Lefty Frizzell. Song highlights: Crazy • I'm Sorry • Making Believe • Wings Of A Dove • Saginaw Michigan • and 16 others.
_____00359509 $8.95

Volume 5
Includes: Merle Travis, Johnny Cash, Grant Turner, Vernon Dalhart, Marty Robbins, Roy Horton, "Little" Jimmie Dickens. 19 selections: Sixteen Tons • Folsom Prison Blues • El Paso • Mockingbird Hill • May The Bird of Paradise.
_____00359512 $8.95

Prices, availability and contents subject to change without notice.
Prices may vary outside the U.S.A.